20 FUN FACTS ABOUT WETLAND HABITATS

BY THERESE M. SHEA

Gareth Stevens
PUBLISHING

Please visit our website, www.garethstevens.com. For a free color catalog of all our high-quality books, call toll free 1-800-542-2595 or fax 1-877-542-2596.

Library of Congress Cataloging-in-Publication Data

Names: Shea, Therese, author.
Title: 20 fun facts about wetland habitats / Therese M. Shea.
Other titles: Twenty fun facts about wetland habitats
Description: New York : Gareth Stevens Publishing, [2022] | Series: Fun fact file. Habitats | Includes index.
Identifiers: LCCN 2020038026 (print) | LCCN 2020038027 (ebook) | ISBN 9781538264591 (library binding) | ISBN 9781538264577 (paperback) | ISBN 9781538264584 (6 pack) | ISBN 9781538264607 (ebook)
Subjects: LCSH: Wetland ecology–Juvenile literature. | Wetland biodiversity–Juvenile literature.
Classification: LCC QH541.5.M3 S486 2022 (print) | LCC QH541.5.M3 (ebook) | DDC 577.68–dc23
LC record available at https://lccn.loc.gov/2020038026
LC ebook record available at https://lccn.loc.gov/2020038027

First Edition

Published in 2022 by
Gareth Stevens Publishing
29 East 21st Street
New York, NY 10010

Designer: Michael Flynn
Editor: Kate Mikoley

Photo credits: Cover, p. 1 (main) Edwin Remsberg/The Image Bank/Getty Images; file folder used throughout David Smart/Shutterstock.com; binder clip used throughout luckyraccoon/Shutterstock.com; wood grain background used throughout ARENA Creative/Shutterstock.com; p. 5 John Stewart/The Image Bank/Getty Images; p. 6 gnagel/iStock/Getty Images; p. 7 (fen) Dneutral Han/Moment/Getty Images; p. 7 (bog) geogif/iStock/Getty Images; p. 8 (marsh) Cynthia Farr-Weinfeld/Moment/Getty Images; p. 8 (swamp) Mike Wёwerka/500px Prime/Getty Images; p. 10 Larry Mayer/Stockbyte/Getty Images; p. 11 Zeiss4Me/E+/Getty Images; p. 12 Good_Stock/iStock/Getty Images; p. 13 Boris SV/Moment/Getty Images; p. 14 TorriPhoto/Moment Open/Getty Images; p. 15 (pitcher plant) benedek/iStock/Getty Images; p. 15 (sundew) Naturfoto/Corbis Documentary/Getty Images; p. 16 (Florida panther) Art Wolfe/Stone/Getty Images; p. 16 (whooping crane) jferrer/iStock/Getty Images; p. 17 Lagunatic-Photo/iStock/Getty Images; p. 18 KenCanning/E+/Getty Images; p. 19 Chase Dekker Wild-Life Images/Moment/Getty Images; p. 20 Ivan Murauyou/iStock/Getty Images; p. 21 Raul Rodriguez/iStock/Getty Images; p. 22 Tang Chhin Sothy/AFP/Getty Images; p. 23 Thinkstock/Stockbyte/Getty Images; p. 24 Marty Watson/EyeEm/Getty Images; p. 25 crix/iStock/Getty Images; p. 26 DennisTangneyJr/iStock/Getty Images; p. 27 https://en.wikipedia.org/wiki/World_Wetlands_Day#/media/File:World_Wetlands_Day_in_Pakistan.jpg; p. 29 Tetra Images/Getty Images.

Printed in the United States of America

Some of the images in this book illustrate individuals who are models. The depictions do not imply actual situations or events.

CPSIA compliance information: Batch #CSGS22: For further information contact Gareth Stevens, New York, New York at 1-800-542-2595.

CONTENTS

What Are Wetlands? 4

A Number of Names 6

Where's the Water? 10

Plenty of Wetland Plants 13

Essential Animal Habitat 16

Wetlands in Trouble 20

Why We Need Wetlands 22

Wonderful Wetlands 27

Glossary. 30

For More Information 31

Index 32

Words in the glossary appear in **bold** type the first time they are used in the text.

WHAT ARE WETLANDS?

When it rains where you live, where does the water go? Does it disappear into the soil? Does it collect on top, filling up the ground like a pool?

Wetlands are places where the soil is covered with **shallow** water at least part of the year. The water may be fresh, salty, or a mix. Some wetlands are on the coast. Tides carry water over them. Others are inland, sometimes near flooding rivers and lakes. All wetlands are important to animals, plants—and people too!

Wetlands are often saturated, or filled with water. The water doesn't move around much.

A NUMBER OF NAMES

THERE ARE MORE THAN 20 NAMES FOR WETLANDS!

People in different places call different wetlands different names. These include marshes, estuaries, mangroves, mudflats, mires, fens, swamps, deltas, coral reefs, billabongs, lagoons, shallow seas, bogs, muskegs, sloughs, peatlands, potholes, pocosins, playas, vernal pools, and floodplains.

All wetlands are areas where water doesn't drain, or flow out, easily.

BOGS AND FENS ARE WETLANDS MADE OF DYING PLANTS!

Four main wetland groups are swamps, marshes, bogs, and fens. All have different soil and plant life. Bogs and fens have peat, a spongy matter made of slowly dying plants. They form over thousands of years.

FEN

BOG

The moss in bogs can grow in the low-**nutrient**, low-oxygen soil. Fens can have a bit more plant life because their water sources have more nutrients.

IF THE WETLAND HAS A LOT OF TREES, IT'S A SWAMP!

Swamps and marshes have richer soil than bogs and fens.
You can tell a marsh and a swamp apart because trees and
other woody plants grow in swamps.

SWAMP

MARSH

Marshes might have a few trees, but
they mostly have grassy plants.

WETLAND GROUPS

KIND	SOIL	COMMON PLANTS	LOCATION	KIND OF WATER
SWAMP	MANY NUTRIENTS	TREES	LOW, FLAT AREAS NEAR RIVERS AND COASTS	FRESHWATER OR SALTWATER SOURCES
MARSH	MANY NUTRIENTS	GRASSES, SEDGES	LOW, FLAT AREAS NEAR RIVERS AND COASTS	FRESHWATER OR SALTWATER SOURCES
BOG	ACIDIC, FEW NUTRIENTS	MOSSES	WHERE GLACIERS DUG OUT HOLES IN EARTH	FRESH WATER (RAIN OR SNOW ONLY)
FEN	LESS ACIDIC, MORE NUTRIENTS THAN BOGS	GRASSES, SEDGES, WILDFLOWERS	WHERE GLACIERS DUG OUT HOLES IN EARTH	FRESH WATER (MOSTLY GROUNDWATER)

Many different factors can help us decide what kind of wetland an area is.

WHERE'S THE WATER?

NOT ALL WETLANDS ARE FOUND NEAR BODIES OF WATER.

Some wetlands are found in depressions, or areas that are lower than the land around them. However, they aren't near oceans, rivers, or lakes. Their water comes from water under the ground, rain, or **runoff**.

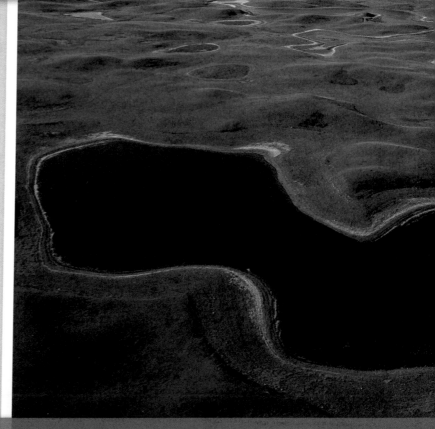

Wetlands that form in depressions away from water sources we can see are sometimes called prairie potholes.

Wetlands that are dry part of the year often have sturdy plants such as trees.

SOME WETLANDS ARE DRY AT TIMES.

Some wetlands depend on rainfall or runoff and can dry up. Some are seasonal, which means they form when **precipitation** arrives with a certain season. Droughts, or long periods without rain, can also dry up wetlands.

11

There is 1,000 times more water in the earth than in all rivers and lakes! Groundwater is part of the water cycle, the way in which water moves around Earth.

FUN FACT: 6

SOME WETLANDS EXIST BECAUSE UNDERGROUND WATER RISES.

Groundwater is water that's below Earth's surface. It's found in soil and rocky earth. Sometimes this water is quite near the surface, like that under some wetlands. Deeper waters may be underground for thousands of years!

PLENTY OF WETLAND PLANTS

ABOUT 5,000 SPECIES, OR KINDS, OF PLANTS LIVE IN U.S. WETLANDS.

Cattails are common wetland plants. They're an important food source for wetland animals. Every part of the plant can be eaten.

Some wetland plants live totally underwater. Others float. Still others are rooted underwater and grow out of the water. What wetland plant species live where depends on the water content and whether the water dries up.

13

IF YOU LICKED A MANGROVE LEAF, IT MIGHT TASTE SALTY!

Mangroves are types of trees and shrubs, or bushes, that are found in warm coastal wetlands. They can grow in salt water. Their roots remove salt. Mangroves may also get rid of salt through their leaves.

Mangroves can live in water 100 times saltier than many other plants can handle.

SOME WETLAND PLANTS EAT BUGS!

Bog soil is missing nutrients many kinds of plants need. Special **adaptations** help some plants live in bogs, though. Pitcher plants and sundews get nutrients by catching and eating bugs!

PITCHER PLANT

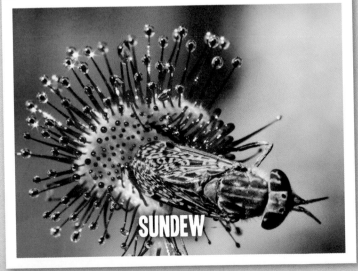

SUNDEW

Sundews catch bugs with their sticky parts. Pitcher plants catch bugs in their "pitcher," which is filled with a special liquid to break bugs down into nutrients.

15

ESSENTIAL ANIMAL HABITAT

MORE THAN 40 PERCENT OF ENDANGERED OR THREATENED ANIMAL SPECIES IN THE UNITED STATES NEED WETLANDS.

The whooping crane is an endangered wetland bird. The Florida panther is a kind of mountain lion that lives in wetland **habitats**. There are fewer than 150 left.

WHOOPING CRANE

FLORIDA PANTHER

The Florida panther's population has gone down as its habitat has been taken away for people's use.

Alligators may make small holes in wetlands using their feet, noses, and tails. These holes hold water during dry times and provide a home for small wetland animals.

WETLANDS ARE LIKE RESTAURANTS FOR ANIMALS!

Plant leaves, stems, and other parts decompose, or break down, in wetland waters. The results are tiny bits of food that small wetland bugs, fish, and shellfish can eat. Then, these animals become food for bigger animals.

17

WETLANDS ARE A REST STOP FOR MIGRATING BIRDS!

Species of birds that migrate sometimes travel thousands of miles. Wetlands provide places to rest, hide from predators, and find food. It's believed that about one-third of all bird species need wetlands to live.

All wild ducks and geese in the United States depend on wetlands for a place to live, find food, and raise families.

Beavers may live in the dams they build. They may also build a separate home near the dam called a lodge.

FUN FACT: 13

BEAVERS CREATE SOME WETLANDS!

Beavers make dams across streams and rivers. They construct the dams out of fallen trees, branches, mud, and rocks. By blocking running water, they create a pond to call home—and they create wetlands too.

19

WETLANDS IN TROUBLE

FUN FACT: 14

TODAY'S CONTINENTAL UNITED STATES ONCE HAD ABOUT 220 MILLION ACRES (89 MILLION HA) OF WETLANDS.

Scientists think about half of those wetlands have disappeared over the past 500 years. People aren't the only cause of this. However, they have done a lot of harm.

Some scientists believe that more than 60 percent of the world's wetlands have disappeared since 1900.

THREATS TO WETLANDS

MAN-MADE THREATS

- USING LANDS FOR CROPS AND RAISING ANIMALS
- CHANGING WATERWAYS, SUCH AS WITH DAMS, CANALS, AND OTHER CONSTRUCTION
- FILLING IN OR DRAINING LANDS TO MAKE ROOM FOR HOUSES AND OTHER BUILDINGS
- CREATING AIR AND WATER POLLUTION

NATURAL THREATS

- RISING SEA LEVELS
- STORMS SUCH AS HURRICANES

Most threats to wetlands come from human activity. People can make changes to help keep wetlands around.

WHY WE NEED WETLANDS

WETLANDS CAN STOP FLOODS!

When rivers and lakes flood, wetlands absorb, or take in, floodwaters. They can stop floods from reaching places where people live. Just 1 acre (0.4 ha) of wetland can hold 1 million gallons (3.8 million L) of water!

Some people want to fill in or drain wetlands so they can build on them. However, wetlands are a natural way to defend, or guard, against flooding.

A terrible hurricane hit New Orleans, Louisiana, in 2005. Scientists believe wetlands that had been ruined before the hurricane could have slowed it. People are trying to bring the wetlands back.

WETLANDS CAN SLOW HURRICANES!

Hurricanes are storms with powerful winds and a lot of rain. They need warm ocean water to remain strong. When hurricanes cross coastal wetlands, they usually weaken and do less harm on land.

WETLANDS ARE LIKE A WASTEWATER TREATMENT PLANT!

Wetland soil and plants act like a kind of water filter, or something that removes unwanted things. When polluted water runs through wetlands, it's cleaned and the pollution can get buried. Wetlands keep these bits of pollution from reaching lakes, rivers, and oceans.

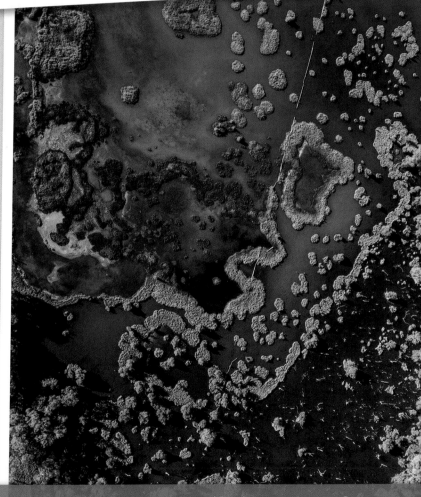

Wetlands clean water that people end up drinking later. Too much pollution can kill the plants and animals of a wetland, though.

When a mangrove forest like this is cut down, carbon dioxide is released, or let go. Mangrove forests store 10 times more carbon than forests on dry land!

FUN FACT: 18

WETLANDS FIGHT CLIMATE CHANGE!

Plants, especially those in wetlands, store a gas called carbon dioxide. Too much of this gas around Earth is a cause of climate change, which is a long-term change in the planet's usual weather patterns. Climate change affects all life on Earth.

25

One way people gather cranberries is by flooding a bog in which they grow. The cranberries float to the water's surface after being knocked off the vine.

WETLANDS PROVIDE US WITH A LOT OF FOOD.

Foods such as cranberries, rice, and blueberries grow well in wetlands. Fish and shellfish that people eat are found there too. Some kinds of **medicine** are made from things in wetland soil and plants.

WONDERFUL WETLANDS

FEBRUARY 2 IS WORLD WETLANDS DAY.

These children in Oman, a country in the Middle East, celebrate World Wetlands Day with special activities, such as coloring.

On February 2, 1971, a group of scientists from different countries came together to try to save wetlands. Now, this special day is marked by events to teach people about the importance of wetlands.

Governments protect some wetlands today. For example, Everglades National Park in Florida contains different kinds of wetlands. However, about three-fourths of all U.S. wetlands are found on the lands owned by American citizens. It's up to these people to keep them healthy.

Perhaps the biggest threat to wetlands around the world is that many people don't realize their value for animals, plants, and the water supply. It's up to all of us to spread the news that wetlands are important!

Even though much of the Everglades is a national park, these wetlands still face dangers. Hurricanes, pollution, and a decreasing water supply are a few.

GLOSSARY

acidic: having the properties of an acid, a liquid that breaks down matter

adaptation: a change in a type of animal or plant that makes it better able to live in its surroundings

continental: having to do with the part of the United States that's made up of the lower 48 states (without Alaska or Hawaii)

endangered: in danger of dying out

habitat: the natural place where an animal or plant lives

medicine: a drug taken to make a sick person well

migrate: to move to warmer or colder places for a season. Also, to move from one area to another for feeding or having babies.

nutrient: something a living thing needs to grow and stay alive

precipitation: rain, snow, sleet, or hail

runoff: water from rain or snow that flows over land into a body of water

sedge: a plantlike grass with a triangular stem that grows in wet ground or near water

shallow: not deep

threatened: likely to become endangered, or in danger of dying out

FOR MORE INFORMATION

BOOKS

Best, B. J. *Wetlands.* New York, NY: Cavendish Square Publishing, 2018.

Sidabras, Kimberly. *Wetlands.* Philadelphia, PA: Mason Crest, 2019.

Willis, John. *Wetlands.* New York, NY: AV2, 2021.

WEBSITES

Wetlands

animals.sandiegozoo.org/habitats/wetlands

Read about some animals and plants found in wetlands.

What Is a Wetland?

oceanservice.noaa.gov/facts/wetland.html

Watch a short video about wetlands.

INDEX

animals 4, 13, 16, 17, 21, 24, 28

billabongs 6

birds 16, 18

bogs 6, 7, 8, 9, 15, 26

bugs 15, 17

carbon dioxide 25

coast 4, 9, 14, 23

coral reefs 6

deltas 6

estuaries 6

Everglades 28, 29

fens 6, 7, 8, 9

floodplains 6

floods 22

groundwater 9, 12

hurricanes 21, 23, 29

lagoons 6

lakes 4, 10, 13, 22, 24

mangroves 6, 14, 25

marshes 6, 7, 8, 9

mires 6

mosses 7, 9

mudflats 6

muskegs 6

nutrients 7, 9, 15

oceans 10, 23, 24

peat 7

peatlands 6

plants 4, 7, 8, 9, 11, 13, 14, 15, 17, 24, 25, 26, 28

playas 6

pocosins 6

pollution 21, 24, 29

potholes 6, 10

rain 4, 9, 10, 11, 23

rivers 4, 9, 10, 13, 19, 22, 24

runoff 10, 11

shallow seas 6

sloughs 6

soil 4, 7, 8, 9, 12, 24, 26

swamps 6, 7, 8, 9

tides 4

trees 8, 9, 11, 19

United States 16, 18, 20, 28

vernal pools 6

water cycle 12

World Wetlands Day 27